Table of Contents

Introduction

This is the first in a series of my e-books, the rest of which will be available shortly.

How many times has someone said, "I love my home but I'm tired of the way it looks... It feels dated... It seems cluttered... It appears so disjointed"? "I'm just not happy, but I don't know how or even where to ever begin to make changes."

Well, you are not alone. Everybody has said that at least once in their life! Sometimes each day, as you look around you, telling yourself, "I have to make some changes here!" and month after month, even year after year, you just keep putting off tackling even the smallest change. Or maybe you just keep adding to your home, ultimately realizing, "I've got too much stuff and I'm just so bored and tired of it all!"

It can seem overwhelming, especially because most of the time we are not even sure what exactly it IS that bothers us the most. The only thing you do know is that when you look around you, you aren't happy in your surroundings. "I just need somebody to tell me what is wrong and where I should begin to fix it."

There are so many items that make up a home's décor that what many people are lacking is a simple way to begin the process of examining the possible things at fault.

Ultimately by going over the chapters in this book, you will be simply and clearly directed to answers as to WHAT is bothering you about your décor and then the steps you can take to make the pertinent decisions you need to bring you the home décor you really desire.

It will pare down distractions, help you to focus on problem areas, and come to conclusions so you can begin to transform your home into a place of comfort, pleasure and pride. Below are the questions you need to ask yourself before you do anything else.

What is your décor "style"?

Perhaps you are ready for an entirely different style than you have had for the last many years and are now ready to make the leap to a new you and an entirely different look for your home. For example, maybe you currently have a Traditional look but have been yearning for a less-cluttered, Transitional, or soft Contemporary style?

Or possibly your style is not the problem because you love your style just as it is, whether it is Traditional, Modern, etc.; but still, something is just not making you happy with your décor. You know that something needs tweaking.

"Hmm," you keep thinking. "Why am I not thrilled with my home's décor?"

Maybe the furniture <u>itself</u> is bothering you?

As mentioned above, perhaps you are okay with your style. It could be you are just tired of your old furniture. Give it some thought since you still like your older furniture and the style it all conveys; but it may be that your unhappiness with your look is simply that the furniture feels old and dated and needs a "face-lift."

Maybe the problem is simply the furniture <u>arrangement</u>?

Think about the arrangement of your furniture, especially the core pieces. Could it be that the furniture just needs to be rearranged or pared down? Take a good look. It could be that the arrangement is stale or impractical or awkward.

Do you have too much furniture? It is not at all uncommon for most of us to eventually segue to an issue of too much of a good thing. We can't rid ourselves of favorite pieces, whether heirlooms or cherished items or simply bargains we couldn't resist. And before you know it, after years of adding pieces here and there, it's a discombobulated mix of pieces that, while individually you love each one, all together has become just too much.

When this happens, nothing stands out as each piece overshadows the other and there is no focal piece, no wow, no balance and harmony.

Could it be that maybe you just need a new <u>color palette</u> entirely or need to incorporate a new color into your décor?

Okay; maybe you still LOVE your STYLE, but you're bored with or tired of your current color palette. For example, maybe you did your home in all neutrals but now you're tired of it and want color in your life. Or maybe just the reverse! You always loved color but now want most of your pieces done in neutral for a more calming feel. Or maybe what would make you happy is doing mostly neutral pieces but with color just as accents.

Perhaps your home feels <u>cluttered</u> with too many little chachkies?

But you love all your little collections, your collectibles. It's who you are! Okay, but often it gets to the point that all these little treasures seem to take over the room or your home and they begin closing in on you. Could this be the whole crux of your problem?

Perhaps you simply need to declutter, to let go of some accessories (or a lot of them!), or rearrange these treasured pieces you've been adding to your home for years. Your home can still exude you and your personality but in a more organized, and a "less is more," way.

How to Make a Change

My goodness; a lot of things to take into consideration. Just how does one begin to make a change?

Well, in this book, I am going to give you the answers. The points above should get you thinking and help you get started in narrowing down what it IS about your space that isn't working for you. Maybe the problem is just one of the above, maybe two, or maybe all! Perhaps it's a little this and a little that. Our homes over all the years tend to literally become a "little this and a little that" which culminates in our frustration.

This will explain an easy 7-step process that ANYONE can follow, to simply help you figure out: WHAT do I need to change and where do I START?

In the chapters that follow, you will quickly get to that starting point you've been yearning for. They will help you answer your own questions about what it is that you don't like about your décor. You have already taken the first step, by beginning to take a few minutes to read this simple guide.

When finished, you will have more confidence in the decisions you need in order to start making changes, whether big or small, that transform your home into your vision, a home exuding your unique personality while at the same time reflecting a comfortable, beautiful, organized space, put together in a way that will bring you peace and tranquility and satisfaction for many years to come.

Chapter 1: Budget

Unless you win the lottery, most likely your budget will dictate, at least in part, what you are able to change or how much or even the time frame you are able to do this change. Most people need to prioritize, as well as decide whether they can make only small changes or go all out!

But do not fret. Decorating changes can always be made, no matter how small a budget. For instance, if all you need is a couple of pieces recovered, don't hesitate to get quotes from upholsterers, as everyone is offering lower prices nowadays. The same is true for getting one or two new pieces of furniture. You'd be amazed at how inexpensive you can buy certain new pieces today. Often, retailers are offering 50% off daily with sales up to 75% off!

And don't discount flea markets and garage sales. These can provide some real finds – even things you wouldn't find in a regular discount store today. There are a lot of treasures at these kinds of places, more than there used to be. As the economy dips, vendors at flea markets will often barter more than they used to.

As many Americans find themselves downsizing today, garage sales can be a goldmine of bargains. And don't forget consignment stores! I have found so many great pieces, and at fabulous prices at these stores. Just keep checking and revisiting them. Patience pays off! They are also a great avenue to sell off your old pieces too. Even thrift stores have some great pieces for pennies on the dollar.

And don't forget places like Craig's List to help rid your home of pieces you are willing to let go of. It's a fast way to help de-clutter, whether it's furniture items you want to sell or even accessories. All of it can be sold on Craig's List. And the best part is it's an extremely user-friendly site, very easy to learn if you haven't experienced working with it in the past.

New accessories are certainly obtainable even if you can't afford new furniture, as they are certainly the smallest budget items and they can be extremely inexpensive at discount places as well as flea markets. I've even had much luck with some real treasures at places like Salvation Army's thrift store!

Remember, depending on your budget size, you still need to decide what will give you the biggest bang for your buck.

Things to ask yourself include: HOW MUCH can you spend? How much do you WANT to spend? What is your TIME FRAME?

Chapter 2: Is Your Problem That You Need a "*New Style*"?

Collect magazine photos, etc.; photos from wherever you can, for that matter. Start a file folder called "Styles That I Like." Cut out pictures of everything having to do with home décor, not just furniture. Cut out pillows you like, accessories you are drawn to, art on the walls, rugs, chandeliers and other lights and lamps, fabrics you fall in love with, paint colors.

Just keep adding to your file and pour over them. Weed out some too as time goes on as you'll see that what you loved last month is now replaced with different items. Ah yes, this is a huge part of the problem – we all can be very fickle.

Another helpful tool that's fun to do is to create a "vision board." For this you merely need to have a large cardboard or canvas board where you can tape photos of your favorite pieces. You could even use a photograph board or a corkboard to attach your photos and fabric swatches, etc. As you narrow them down, you will see how everything is unfolding; and all of this will help you to envision what your home will appear like when finished.

This board will be a work in progress the entire time you are "researching" which direction you wish to go. But if you can't seem to find a board to do a vision board, a file folder will do just fine.

Also, go through model homes. Peruse through furniture stores, all kinds, to see what you like. It's equally important to weed out what you DON'T like, too! Give this time. Don't just do it over a weekend or even over a month! Remember, you are trying to ascertain a trend of the style you are gravitating towards by taking your time to review these sources. If you do this thoroughly, you should begin to see an obvious pattern of the style you are leaning towards.

But wait; sometimes there is a dilemma that occurs in this research process. You just can't decide! You love them all! Don't give up – take your time. We are all so inspired by everything around us that often we decide to redo a room, or our entire home, too quickly just because we saw a friend's new décor, or saw a sofa in a store we like, or something in a magazine, and boom! We are off and running! Cha ching, cha ching!

We want it NOW and then guess what? Sometimes while things are even still on order, we start having doubts. Uh oh, hmm; now I'm not sure if that really IS the look I want. Maybe I acted to hastily....

So again, define your style, taking your time to do it. Some examples of popular styles are:

- Traditional
- Contemporary
- Transitional (not quite contemporary, but not quite traditional)
- Mediterranean
- Spanish
- Moroccan
- Asian
- Tropical
- Colonial
- Arts and Crafts
- Coastal
- Cottage
- English Tudor
- Shabby Chic

Or, a mix of a couple of the above!

Sometimes you might be drawn to a couple of very different styles and looks. "Hmm, how do I choose just one particular style when I love two of them?" you might say. No worries. Nowadays, it's not at all uncommon to mix styles for what we call an "eclectic" look.

For example, you yearn for a cleaner, soft, Contemporary style, but you still have a lot of Traditional pieces you need to tie in. You still love some of the antique tables or mirrors or chairs you've collected (or inherited) but you really are also leaning towards a soft Contemporary look. No problem! Contemporary combined with antiques can look beautiful together!

How to make it work? Simply make sure you mix both styles

thoroughly throughout your entire home so there's a nice balance of the two looks, making sure you continue the same color scheme throughout your entire home to unite your mix of styles. Keep in mind to do this carefully and blend the different styles so they come together as a well-thought-out beautiful, unique look that simply defies definition. But, in actuality, it is called "eclectic"!

Let's look at some style examples.

Transitional Style

Transitional style can become an elegant bedroom. In other words, the beautiful headboard isn't Contemporary but it's not entirely Traditional either. It's a mix we call "Transitional."

The color palette is neutral, beiges on creams. Note the textures that add coziness with the pillows.

All you need to do to mix it up is change your flowers on the dresser!

Mediterranean Style

This is an example of a classic Italian, or Mediterranean, style. Notice how everything is kept rich and dark – from the furniture, rug, and fabrics to the art, lamp bases and centerpiece bowl.

This is a very common Italian style that would be beautiful carried throughout the home. But if you were tired of it, you could simply reupholster the chairs, get new accessories, including lamp shades, and you'll have an entirely different Italian look.

Imagine deep red upholstered chairs, lampshades in mustard, reds and greens, and a green Italian bowl filled with lemons as a centerpiece. A brand new look!

Old World Style

This is pure Old World style, especially with the furniture design. What makes it pop is the fun color palette. Here is used a combination of four colors … orange/red, green, white, and grey.

It displays an inviting blend of patterns in the fabrics, but which are coordinated with the color palette, so it all goes together like the pieces of a puzzle.

Note how the accessories, even on the back wall, all contribute to reinforcing this color scheme.

Coastal Style

This is a nice example of a Coastal style ... casual and inviting. The color palette can be all soft colors (think pastels) or bright (think turquoise and orange) or a combination.

What really makes it Coastal is your fabric(s) and accessories. Here you see rattan, complemented with Coastal prints in the accent chair and pillow; and don't forget the accessories. Throw in a few shells and you've got Coastal – as long as your fabrics exude that and you keep within a Coastal color palette.

You don't even need to use rattan furniture. You can use a traditional sofa and just use throw pillows with a Coastal theme. Easy breezy!

Modern Style

This is a true Modern design. Very clean lines, simple edges, often combined with stainless, metallic finishes, shag or geometric rugs, and often a primary color palette.

Chapter 3: Color Scheme

This is going to have a huge impact. The color (or lack of) is what the eyes see first when you walk into a home or a room. Often the "style" you choose will dictate, or narrow down, your color choices, which can be a good thing. Sometimes the choices out there today are so plentiful that it overwhelms you and freezes you from deciding which direction is best to proceed. But some styles naturally gravitate toward tried and true color palettes that are definite winners.

For example, if you are doing Mediterranean, popular color schemes are reds, greens and yellows, of all different hues and shades. But you probably wouldn't use hot pink! If you are doing a Coastal look, you may not want to incorporate a bright purple (although a soft lavender could work very well). Coastal often is shown with cool ocean colors such as light blues, soft sea foam greens, seashell soft pinks, etc.

Quite often, a color scheme can be one of the very things that is making you unhappy with your home's décor. Maybe you started years ago with your LIVING ROOM in soft green and red florals but the more casual FAMILY ROOM somehow ended up being done in green and blue plaids (with maybe some leather), and the powder room is still painted the peach color from when you bought the home years ago, while the kitchen is painted its original bland yellow color. You keep thinking, "I just don't feel comfortable in these rooms. It's all disjointed. Why doesn't it make me happy?"

The answer oftentimes is that there are too many colors going on and there is no continuity. Maybe each room is a mishmash of different colors. Sure you love all the different colors and you may love each room separately; but as you go about your day going from room to room, you just feel like something's wrong with the décor.

Well maybe you simply need to do what the experts do. Pick a color palette and stick with it throughout your entire home. Typically a good palette is three colors, with possibly a fourth as an accent color. A distinct color palette will actually make a lot of your decisions easier for you; but more importantly, it unifies each room to the other. Your entire home will flow much better.

A good, distinct, limited color palette that is consistent everywhere you look will make even the most mishmashed décor come together better. For instance, even with an eclectic mix of furniture, as long as you stick with a particular color palette throughout the entire home, everything will look more unified, more balanced, more professional, and more pleasing to the eye.

But remember, don't start painting yet. Just because you love a couple of different colors, keep in mind that you need to play with how these will work together, and look in different lighting, and if they will compliment your style, etc. Right now, you are just getting inspirations and thinking about what your palette should be.

You're thinking, getting samples, and adding them to your folder or onto your vision board. Take home paint chips and see how they look during different times of the day, as they will change with the natural light and your own lighting. You are only in the "deciding what to do" phase. Get the small sample paint cans even. Just don't paint wall after wall.

Ultimately, though, you will pick your three colors and incorporate only these three colors as your main colors in each and every room. Simply put, you won't believe what a change just this alone will make! Think about it. When you go into model homes, every single one of them does this design rule.

For example, you walk through the door and bam! Living room is done in a sage green, eggplant and cream palette. Maybe the walls are sage green in the living room, the sofa is cream with sage green and eggplant (and soft lavender, as it is in the eggplant family!) pillows, while an occasional chair is upholstered in a sage green, eggplant, lavender and cream plaid and another chair is in sage green.

And guess what; as you walk through the rest of the home, maybe the kitchen walls are cream but the counter stools are sage green and the dining room is painted a soft plum with dining chairs upholstered in a cream and sage green floral, while the powder room is painted a dramatic dark eggplant.

And all the accessories either fall into this color palette too or are a neutral, natural, earthy color. As you walk through the rest of the house, this color palette will follow with everything, everywhere. The bathrooms will be done in the same color palette: the bedroom's linens, duvet, even drapery … everything is unified. This little trick alone gives any home instant continuity and a wow power!

Here are some color scheme examples.

Transitional Color Scheme

A very bold and striking, but comfortable, style. This is a Transitional look. That is, it's not Traditional and it's also not Contemporary. It's an in between style.

It shows a mix of furniture designs; but what makes it really stand out is the color palette – only three colors: white, black, and yellow. If you carried this palette throughout your home, imagine how fun and striking it would be.

I would follow this up with an espresso or black dining table with white upholstered chairs, and yellow and white candlesticks, etc., on the dining table top. You COULD even add a fourth color, red, to this palette if desired. Gorgeous!

Old World Color Scheme

This bed exudes Old World style. The artwork on the bed is so simple but significant that this is an example of where you want to keep your color scheme within the colors on this bed.

Note how by doing this, everything complements each other and everything just simply goes with each other. It takes the guesswork out of what your color palette should be. Sometimes it's right there in front of you!

Spring Colors Color Scheme

Here is a beautiful example of a Spring Colors palette or color scheme. Colors of crisp white, fuscia and pinks, along with fresh spring green just seem to beckon you. Note the great mix of solids along with prints. Just the perfect balance of detail. Who doesn't love this? So happy and inviting.

See how even the accessories pick up the palette. This style is an Old World, Traditional look but, as with any palette, these colors could be used on ANY style, i.e. Contemporary, Cottage Style, etc. Just make sure to carry the same palette throughout your home and pull in accessories that emphasize your STYLE.

Coastal Color

Here's an excellent example of a coastal color palette. It conveys soft, neutral, calm. An easy blend of sand colors, aquas, pinks and light blues. Note the linen/burlap textures. Can't you just smell the beach breezes?

Chapter 4: Furniture Decisions

Scenario One – But I STILL LOVE My OLD Furniture!

You are happy with your current style but are tired of your furniture, PLUS you can't afford to buy any new furniture anyway!

If you are loving your style and don't want to change that, but the furniture pieces just seem old and worn and need to be brought back to life, you have two choices: slipcovers or new fabrics.

Slipcovers can be a lifesaver if you are dealing with a minimal budget or little time. There are a lot of beautiful, and inexpensive, slipcovers available today that can be easily enhanced with some new pillows for an overall huge change, even if this is all you do! It's like a facelift for your furniture.

The best part is that most slipcovers are readily returnable (especially at places like Bed, Bath & Beyond), so you can easily take them for a "test drive," playing with different ones and different styles, maybe trying some new pillows as well. And voila! This alone may do the trick for very little money!

At the very least, if you were thinking of changing your fabric, say on the sofa, to a different solid, and simply want to see how it might look with your existing pillows, or new ones, by trying a slipcover FIRST, it'll take some of the guesswork out of how your sofa will look in your room with the new color(s) you are contemplating. It's an inexpensive way to give you a visual.

If slipcovers don't work, reupholstering is your next option. Often, just by reupholstering, it feels like you have new furniture! It can even make you feel like you have a brand new room!

You will need to begin collecting ideas for new fabrics with which to reupholster your certain pieces, albeit still focusing on retaining that particular style you currently have. This is where some people get tripped up. There are so many fabrics to choose from that sometimes we end up buying yards of a new fabric that we have fallen for, have a piece reupholstered, only to end up saying it STILL doesn't look right in this room!

Too often people don't buy the CORRECT fabric for their style. So then, after spending all their time and money, the newly-upholstered piece is all wrong for the room. Here is an example. You meant to still stay with a Traditional style, but now that it's all reupholstered, it turned out looking too Contemporary! It now doesn't "go" with your other pieces that you wanted it to coordinate with.

Don't let yourself fall into this trap. Take time to carefully choose what complements and goes with all your other current pieces ... UNLESS you actually are changing your style completely!

Scenario Two – I'm READY for NEW Furniture!

You love your style but are ready to purchase some new furniture to refresh your look.

OK, you are keeping your current style but can afford to purchase some new pieces to refreshen your look. Just reupholstering is not enough for you at this point. This direction, though, involves quite a few more decisions and time and research.

As you've probably noticed, there is an over-abundance of gorgeous furniture as well as fabric options on the market. Too many choices, actually. Which means you will need to decide on new everything: prints, new colors, maybe even new textures.

But again, remember to stay within your style. And you are on just a fact-finding mission – just get photos and fabric swatches to contemplate for now because you will definitely see how impressionable you can be as you keep searching. You will find an abundance of pieces and fabrics – and you will love them all! So mull over your choices for a good deal of time before any actual purchasing.

Scenario Three – I'm READY for a Totally NEW STYLE!

You want to change your style completely (i.e., you've had a Shabby Chic look but want to change to Contemporary), so you need to dramatically change most of your furniture!

"Yikes!" you might be saying. Well, don't panic.

Now that you know your budget and you know the style you want to change to, plus you are narrowing down your color palette, you are most likely going to need to buy some new pieces of furniture ... or perhaps a lot of new furniture, if you are changing your style completely.

Plan out what new pieces you need to purchase. Once again, flip through many magazines and go through furniture stores, everywhere that gives you ideas. And take your time. If you let yourself be impressionable, it usually ends up as something you wish you hadn't purchased.

As you keep gravitating to certain pieces that you are consistently drawn back to, THEN make sure to do a little drawing of what pieces of furniture you are considering and the possibilities of your furniture placement in whatever room(s) you are changing. You'll find yourself changing this drawing often during this investigation phase. Be sure to use a pencil – with an eraser!

Obviously, most people would want to get away with buying as few pieces as possible to create or complete their desired new look. Given this, the biggest mistake most people make is in buying too big of pieces and too many of them. Measure, measure, measure. It doesn't do all your efforts any good if in the end, yes, you love all your pieces, but they are so crammed in there that you can't function in that room and it's all too cramped!

Remember, your goal is to keep a delicate balance of beauty and function (within your budget!). While furniture is mostly bought for practicality with beauty sometimes coming in a close second, now is your chance to add a new level of beauty and your unique, personal touch to each room.

Now is the time to remember that you don't want to buy a new sofa just because it's on sale or just because your neighbor or best friend bought it.

"But, hey, I love it in their home," you might be saying. Well first of all, that is THEIR place. They've taken their time to create THEIR unique style and look. Copying may be a form of flattery, but we should all know by now that copying your friend's "uniqueness" when she has taken her time and effort to create a "look of her own" is not showing YOUR unique style, touch and personality. It's just going to take the wind out of your friend's sails and show you as being a copycat! So, come on! Put your thinking hat on, work to show who YOU are, think your uniqueness, your talents (not your neighbor's!), and who YOU are so your home, your pieces, your style is all YOURS.

A practical tip to start with is to buy a new sofa that will help with the new look you are going for, that will work even if you change your style again down the road. One that will "go" with a lot of different looks.

Your major pieces are the "anchors" in the room. You will be building around these – for now and in the future. This is really key in all your major furniture pieces now that you have a chance to redo. So no matter what your "style," it's always a good idea to start your basic major furniture pieces (i.e., sofa, etc.) in a somewhat neutral fabric which you can build your style, color, and décor around.

And it's not a bad idea to keep your basic furniture in styles that are timeless and somewhat closer to Transitional. The reason I suggest this is that if you can get it to where your main furniture pieces lean more to a Transitional look, you can easily bring out your favorite style in a way that complements, such as accessories. For example, with a Transitional sofa, if you add pillows with a beautiful Mediterranean tapestry fabric, maybe even tassels, then voila, a Mediterranean look! Add a beautiful Mediterranean motif accent rug and it further enhances the look.

If you buy your major furniture pieces correctly, it will open a whole new world to you. It allows you freedom to change your style in the future – simply by just changing some accessories!

Here are some examples.

Traditional Combined with Transitional

Here is a Traditional sofa design with a Transitional chest on the left. See how the combination works as the different styles are unified with the mirrored Traditional coffee table imitating the mirrored front of the chest.

The color palette here is soft grey blues and soft green and cream, and work well together as these fabric colors are coordinated with the colors in the framed art on the wall. It simplifies mixing different styles together if you just remember to keep everything within your color palette.

An Old World/Contemporary Mix

Here's a perfect example of changing your look. Perhaps you have an older, Old World casual bookcase that you've built an Old World look all around it. You can see here that, just by adding a dramatic Contemporary art piece above it, suddenly you've got a wow effect.

What makes it work? Besides the scale, the colors are coordinated! The wall colors, the bookcase colors and the painting colors – even the orchid colors – all contribute to a dramatic area of your home.

Classic Old World Bed

This classic, Old World bed will never go out of style. What makes it even more inviting is not only the beautiful design but all the textures!

This is a great example of how you can easily change the look and feel of your furniture by adding texture or by changing your color palette. But remember, if you change your palette here, then you need to make sure you add that color throughout your home.

Classic Soft Contemporary Look

Here is a classic soft Contemporary look. With a sectional like this, you could change the look entirely by simply changing the throw pillows and the framed art above the piece.

Many of us have classic pieces that make us feel the room is tired, but try changing the throw pillows and art and a different throw blanket and voila! Your look is entirely different.

In other words, this room could easily transform from Contemporary to Traditional and you would feel like you have new furniture!

More Classic Furniture Tips and Tricks

This is actually an outdoor sectional with a weather-resistant rattan bottom. It has a Contemporary and Tropical feel BUT, guess what; you could really make it look however you want because it's so classic.

If you put Tropical pillows on it, it's Tropical. If you put shell, coral design pillows on it, it's Coastal. If you put on bold Contemporary pillows, it becomes Contemporary!

You could put some beautiful floral or even floral AND plaid/check pillows, and you've got a Traditional look! Plus, you don't just have to use this sectional outside. It's so nice, go ahead and use it indoors. It's a win, win!

Elegant Old World on a Budget

This is a rich, elegant Old World look, beautifully coordinated. But if you had a similar look and were ready for a new look, on a budget, try just changing the upholstery and the artwork, say beige fabrics with red and beige print pillows and artwork with lots of different shades of reds and creams and beige; and maybe put a red bowl with white hydrangeas on the coffee table and, then? Guess what! You have an entirely different room! It's so easy!

Transforming a Traditional Leather Sofa

Many of us have had this Traditional leather sofa style. But take note that by adding an interesting rug and artwork, and keeping the color scheme unified, it comes across as a well put together, inviting room.

The color scheme is kept mostly neutral with a touch of a rusty red for a pop. Note the grey in the sofas is carried through in the grey granite on the coffee table and end tables. Sophisticated look but a casual feel.

Ways to Transform the Look of Your Bed

Although this headboard is similar to a Traditional sleigh bed headboard, the dressers appear to be more of a Transitional look, especially because of their hardware PLUS the duvet and pillows, with their geometric bold Contemporary patterns, appear all together to make this entire overall look a Transitional look.

But if you only just changed the duvet and pillows, you could easily make this many other types of looks. The hardware is subtle enough on the dresser that by doing a different duvet, etc., you could make this any style you'd like.

Chapter 5: Floors

Again, this is all budget determined. But even with a very little budget to work with, huge changes can be made. Small budget? Spruce up with maybe just changing your inexpensive accent or throw rugs. It's acceptable nowadays to even put an area rug on top of a wall-to-wall rug. No problem! Just make sure the design, color and shape add to your look and enhance it.

You want to be careful to not just add an area rug or accent rug for the purpose of adding color. Before doing so, take into consideration the size of the room. Consider what else is in that room or maybe what you are contemplating adding to this room. Adding a colorful rug can sound very fun and cheerful, BUT make sure the end result isn't that it overpowers the room or ends up chopping up your space.

Colorful rugs can add all kinds of personality to a room, and it can even be a great focal point, but you don't want it to have the opposite effect and end up being the elephant in the room. One of the keys for great décor is to make sure everything is balanced.

As for ideas for placement, think entry ways, under coffee tables, under desks in office, in powder rooms, bathrooms, kitchen sink area, under kitchen and dining tables. Think under sofas to unite a seating arrangement.

Even the organic ones such as sisal, jute or sea grass (these are the ones that look like straw or rope) have become very popular for all kinds of décor. Rugs can be an inexpensive way to add design, color, texture and personality to any room or home.

Bigger budget? Think swapping that vinyl floor in your kitchen or bath for porcelain tiles. They have come out with a huge selection of porcelain tiles that actually look like travertine marble; and yet not very pricey. They are available from small to large, and you can be creative about how they are applied in a room. Also, tile stores are offering amazing deals.

Even simply swapping out old carpet with new can make a huge statement, and many carpet stores give you free carpet in numerous rooms if you just buy carpet for one! Changing carpet is a very inexpensive design change that will make an enormous difference in your home's look.

Have you ever looked under old carpet and seen old hardwood floors? Well, it happens often; so go ahead and rip out that carpet to expose the hardwood. Even if the hardwood is old, it's still a valuable thing of beauty that, with a little tender loving care, can be totally restored to its original luster.

Changing out your old carpet or old vinyl, etc., to one of the new laminate "hardwood-looking" floorings can be beautiful. These are often more durable than real hardwood and perfect for high traffic areas or active family living around the house. They don't usually scratch as easily as real wood either.

Even just redoing ONLY your entryway in a beautiful hardwood or laminate will greatly enhance your home's first impression. Bamboo flooring is an extremely popular choice today. It's real bamboo, so it's organic, but often lesser-priced than most real hardwoods.

Also known to be found under carpet is good old cement. Currently, it is considered very chic and high design to rip out that old carpet and have your cement "stained" or even lacquered. This stained cement look doesn't work for every style, of course. But for a Contemporary or Transitional look, it can be quite stunning and extremely low maintenance.

If you have a BIG budget, you can begin to investigate stone floors, slate floors, granite floors, and as mentioned previously, real wood floors. Maybe even out of old barns. Perhaps inlaid with tiles, and mosaics. Hand-hewn is a popular rich look for many styles. Wide-planked, maybe. Obviously, the bigger your budget, the bigger your options for your flooring.

But don't forget – don't purchase anything yet! This is just in the thinking phase like all of these points you are considering. Just get lots of samples, samples, samples, and play with them. Lay them in your rooms, against your furniture, against your existing walls or paint palette. You are simply gathering your samples and doing a "look-see."

Here are some specific flooring examples.

Marble Floors

Marble is a beautiful way to enhance your look. This is probably one of the higher-end choices but gives a clean, upscale feel to any room.

If you don't have the budget to use in larger rooms, it's a nice addition in even a powder room or foyer.

Very sophisticated!

Laminate Floors

Laminate, or likewise, floors, such as Pergo, have a lot to offer. They give the look of wood for a lot less money. Quite affordable.

They also are very forgiving as they tend to not scratch as much as real wood. Check out all the pros and cons before you purchase.

Hardwood Floors

Real hardwood floors add warmth and texture to a home. Nowadays the popular look is wide-planked, staggered, distressed and matte. That all adds up to being more forgiving.

If you can carry it throughout most of your home, all the better. But if not, even in just one larger room, it really makes a statement.

Stone Floors

There's a huge array of stone to choose from. Some slate is actually quite affordable, so do your homework before you cross stone off your list. It also looks great on walls and surrounding a fireplace!

Travertine Floors

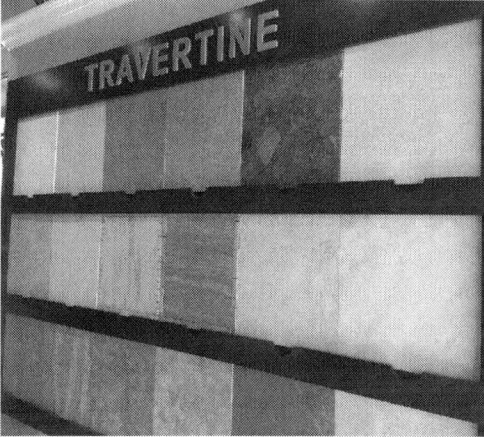

Travertine is another type of marble that has become even more popular over the last decade. It generally has more of a matte look to it, not quite as shiny as formal marble.

It also is quite pricey but worth it if you want to up the elegance and do something different than hardwood. This actually looks outstanding when transitioning to other rooms that perhaps are already done in hardwood floors. It goes well with Modern all the way to Old World looks.

Chapter 6: Window Treatments

Again, as always, keep in mind your budget. Maybe you are leaning toward deciding that all your home needs are some new window treatments to freshen your décor. And some of the lower-budget ideas can be found at discount and hardware stores. You don't have to buy expensive to make a difference.

Besides budget, always remember to keep in mind your style and color palette when contemplating any of these changes.

If lower budget – maybe you currently have metal blinds in some rooms. Just change them out for some simple wooden blinds. This look would go with just about every style. How about bamboo blinds? Equally lovely and will work in a lot of different styles such as Contemporary, Transitional, Tropical, Asian, etc.

For more formal areas or rooms, paneled drapery is obtainable for all budgets and in everything from burlap and linen to satin and silk.

It's easy to find fabulous and inexpensive window treatments of all kinds at a lot of different discount stores. Think Target; Anna's; Bed, Bath & Beyond; and even Wal-Mart. Peruse through all these stores for inspiration as much as you can. Again tear photos from magazines and add all this to your file folder.

Window treatments can be layered as you probably have seen in magazines, etc. For example, sheer drapes behind your thicker, heavier drapes in the front. For a more formal look, have a gorgeous valance made for your space.

For your larger windows, throw in some exquisite tie-backs and you've got a rich layered sophisticated look. Or for smaller windows, think blinds behind your drapery, all giving you some flexibility, options and texture.

And consider the timeless plantation shutters. These will go with practically any look and never go out of style. They give any room a clean, uncluttered look with a lot of practicality from the sun. BUT, if you are in an area that gets a lot of sun and a lot of heat they may need repainting more often, so bear in mind future maintenance for this classic window treatment.

Don't forget, you're still not buying anything! Just getting ideas and taking home samples (or anything with an excellent return policy!) so that you can give yourself a good visual while you are just thinking of what you want to change and how you want to change it. Here are two examples.

Pre-Made Panels Are Inexpensive

We all know the choices for window coverings is endless. Here is an example of one of the best, easiest and cheapest! Pre-made panels are inexpensive and add a great layer of design.

Traditional Valance and Window Treatment

Here is an example of a window treatment combining sheer drapes as well as standard drapes, and all topped off with a traditional valance at the top. This look is a nice touch for any room in your home as this gives you the choice of less or more light in the room and less or more privacy, too.

This window dressing also works for any décor style, whether traditional, modern, etc., simply by changing fabrics and valance style. Your windows, as well as the entire room, will now have more depth and texture. And keep in mind, all can be purchased pre-made at any of the linen stores at bargain prices.

Just think of how, by simply changing your window treatment, you can change the appearance and feel of your whole room!

Chapter 7: Accessories

Ahh, accessories. C'mon, most of us know the power of accessories.

Maybe you have realized THIS is all you need to spruce up your décor! Especially if you are currently dealing with a small budget. A change in accessories can go a long way!

From the moment a friend enters your home, your accessories speak volumes. What greets them in your entryway, or as soon as they come through the door, will set the tone for what they can expect to see throughout the rest of your home. It immediately screams who you are.

Perhaps you have art on the wall or an entry rug or seating in the foyer. Maybe all of this has been left untouched for years. What's bothering you about your home? Could it be simply that you need some new accessories and need to take the time to get rid of a lot of old clutter? Maybe it's time to change the art in the entryway and the throw rug on the floor. You have to start somewhere!

Take time to look around you. I'll bet that if you change a lot of the art on your walls, that alone would make a huge difference. All of this can be bought for very little if you shop discount stores and sales. Now may be the time to replace accessories throughout your entire home.

Think outside the box. Not every wall has to have art on it. It could be a beautiful clock that goes with your new style. There are some really inexpensive clocks made from heavy cardboard that actually work and are like unique art on your wall. This look has lately become really popular. These can be found even at Target or Big Lots, are extremely inexpensive, battery-operated, and typically very light to hang with a single nail.

It's fun to do a small wall entirely in clocks, of all shapes and sizes. Using entirely all cardboard clocks will definitely keep the budget down, but always remember to vary the size and shapes, as you want to do when arranging any accessory, whether on a wall or on a table.

If you can afford a bigger budget, try a clock wall of clocks made of various materials. Some could be cardboard, but others could be wood or even metal. And keep within the "style" of your home. In other words, if your style is old world, you might not want to do a clock wall that includes a very modern clock.

An easy way to look at it is that the goal is the continuity of the subject matter, whether it be clocks, crosses or whatever, while allowing the variety and interest to show through the types, sizes, color and texture. This way your décor flows. It's unified and consistent and your harmony and good taste will simply shine! Plus a focal wall such as this always allows you to have something to collect!

I mean, who doesn't like having something to always look for when shopping?

Or cover an entire wall in crosses. A wall of crosses can really bring out your personality. And it seems you can find all kinds of crosses everywhere nowadays, and at all price points. You could find yourself having as much fun collecting them as you will have hanging them, and another plus is that your friends will always know the perfect gift to give you! Some old antique doors hung on the wall will also make an interesting architectural feature.

Metal wall hangings can be unique and unusual. Some are done in designs that are Italian, some geometric and Contemporary.

Try to keep in mind that walls need not only have art as we know it on them. It is a much more harmonious look to mix your art with other pieces and textures on the walls, all with the goal to bring out your style and personality.

Keep in mind, you must let go of (or pass on to a friend) your old accessories, including art, pillows, etc. You don't want to just keep adding to them. The idea is to get RID of the clutter! Re-think, re-decorate and re-organize.

So, to get started with an accessory change, even the littlest things can make a big statement that your friends and family will certainly notice and enjoy. Go ahead and merely try new throw pillows on your sofas or chairs. Adding these to your older sofa alone can totally change the tone of the room.

Try adding Contemporary pillows on a Traditional sofa if that's all your budget allows; and if, perhaps, you are stuck with the sofa but want a more streamlined, Contemporary look. Same with art on the walls. Swap out your Traditional prints and bring in new Contemporary ones, and notice the huge difference.

Likewise, maybe you have a traditional sofa but want a more Cottage or English look. Keeping in mind your new color palette, you could try adding pillows with, let's say, a cabbage-patch rose design, and maybe throw in some plaid complementary pillows alongside them for a cozy, multi-patterned look.

Just make sure, as always, that the patterns and COLORS are all within your chosen palette. Again, check your magazines for ideas and play with all the photos to help you zone in on your favorites.

Buy some new throw blankets. Toss a new one (making sure it goes with your "new" style and color palette) gracefully over an arm of a sofa, on the back of a chair, draped over an ottoman or gently tossed at the bottom of a bed.

These look cozy and welcoming, especially in cooler weather. Even during warmer weather, they create texture and color and layer your design in the room.

Never forget floral arrangements, plants and even trees. If you have a green thumb, all the better. Small-size florals are great for merely some color and texture and large-size florals offer drama and focal points. If you don't have a green thumb, faux is extremely acceptable nowadays. There are actually some exquisite faux florals that even the most expensive homes show. Target often has a nice selection.

A simple orchid on a coffee table or in a powder room offers a beautiful touch. Twigs in a vase or a pot bring the outdoors in also. Just be sure to add texture and color with different florals that complement your style and décor.

As an example, for Contemporary styles consider adding succulents, for sure! Small ... and especially large, as Contemporary styles command drama. But since these sculptural-style florals come in all sizes, they can go anywhere in your home. These are really popular. (Although any style can incorporate them, they're an especially given fit for Contemporary.)

For Mediterranean, try some lovely olive trees, or even branches. They come in all sizes. Try large for drama or just a small arrangement for texture. Topiaries are a terrific complement for this look, as well.

For Traditional, small ficus trees or branches are perfect complements as either a small arrangement or in vases or large pots. It all depends on your space, budget and style.

Even if all you can spend is around $100, that can go quite far in swapping out some old accessories for new ones. For about that amount of money, if you shop discount (Big Lots, TJ Maxx, Wal-Mart, etc.) you can purchase some new vases, maybe a couple of new throw pillows, and maybe even a new piece of wall art, all obtainable if you buy discount and on sale.

Keep in mind at all times that you are purging your home of unnecessary items to get the full effect of your new look. Sometimes it is extremely helpful to take all artwork or whatever else off all your walls and allow yourself to have a blank canvas to envision the possibilities as you pour through magazines and go through model homes and furniture and accessory stores. This truly is the ideal way to help you reach your goal.

Let's look at some specific accessories and how to use them.

Table Lamps

Table lamps offer an additional opportunity to reflect your style and taste.

Table lamps become another form of accessory as there are unlimited styles to add to your unique look.

An Easy, Inexpensive Mix of Classic Accessories

Here is a perfect example of great accessories and lighting you can find anywhere! The whole grouping works well together as you see how they complement one another.

The lamp is fairly Traditional, the vases are Contemporary, the orchid goes with anything and everything, and the mirror is a Transitional piece, which means it can be incorporated into many different looks and brings a little "bling" to any room.

Note how all these are shown on a Traditional chest but they still complement and "pop" in any room.

Enhancing an Italian-Style Dining Room

Here is a beautiful, traditional Italian-style dining room. If you owned something similar through the years, and are ready for a new look, consider a different type of chandelier, perhaps.

A more wrought-iron piece would make this room more casual. Changing the upholstery will give it a whole new feel.

And changing accessories such as centerpieces and wall pieces can remake the look of any room.

Lighting Accessories

Lighting not only provides function for tasks but also can act as an accessory, giving your room texture and interest.

Traditional Look with a Twist

Here's an overall Traditional look. BUT the twist is the Contemporary large abstract painting over the sofa.

Even though the other wall has Traditional art, it all goes together beautifully. Why? Because the color scheme is united!

The fabric colors on the sofa and pillows are all pulled together with the colors in the large framed art. Likewise the color of the walls, the sisal rug, and the orchid floral all add to integrating the color palette.

Accessories that Complement Each Other

A good design tip is to keep your accessories complementing each other. When displaying various groups of accessories together, mix it up to create balance. In other words, don't have a grouping of all the same size, same shape, same color.

You want to exude variety and texture, all the while staying within your "style." To make the most of your accessories, make your display creative and your personality will shine through it.

Accessories in the Bedroom

Can you see what a huge impact just one piece of art makes in a room over a bed that is neutral?

It's really the same for all rooms. Accessories have a HUGE impact!

Black, Colors, and Accessories

We've all seen classic black leather, whether in a Contemporary style like this or otherwise. But just see how black allows you to really play with color in your accessories.

Here the palette is all the beautiful jewel tones in this fabulous artwork. Spectacular! You could pull those same colors out by using glass vases in the same jewel tones, of various sizes and shapes, on the coffee table for more texture and interest. How dramatic!

Made in the USA
Las Vegas, NV
19 April 2022